THE VISUAL FOREX TRADER©

By Peter Martin Jones

Please be aware that financial spread betting is a leveraged product and can result in losses that exceed your initial deposit.
Spread betting may not be suitable for everyone, so please ensure that you fully understand the risks involved.

TABLE OF CONTENTS

INTRODUCTION

Hello and thank you for purchasing my book. I am sure that you will find this to be a very wise investment and if you follow the simple rules that I will be revealing shortly you will be quickly on your way to making a regular income stream that will change your life forever.

I expect you are maybe slightly sceptical at this stage and I don't blame you. I imagine that perhaps you have tried other Forex schemes in the past and been disappointed with the results – well join the club! So have I. I have wasted thousands of pounds trying out various methods that claim to make you regular large sums of money without success. Don't get me wrong, I don't think that many of these were deliberately misleading but often they don't work for many people for one reason or another.

However, I knew that there were people that do make regular income streams from trading the Forex and I was determined to find a way that worked for me- not just occasionally but consistently and without the involvement of complicated spreadsheets or formulae.

Well I was successful! No more large stopped out losses and a rapidly diminishing bank balance. I am now making regular substantial amounts consistently and living a comfortable lifestyle solely from using my **VISUAL FOREX TRADER** system.

But first things first. We need to make sure that you understand the basics of spread betting and some of the terms involved before we can proceed any further.

WHAT IS SPREAD BETTING

I will briefly explain what spread betting is for those who are not familiar with it. Spread betting allows you to bet, or take a *position*, on whatever you think a financial market will do next. The more the market moves in your favour, the more you profit, with unlimited potential. Conversely, the more the market moves against you, the more you could lose – and you may lose more than your initial deposit. So you must be very careful.

If you are totally new to spread betting, the link below will take you the IG Index video which explains the concept quite well and I strongly recommend you watch this video first. The link is:

http://www.igindex.co.uk/spread-betting/about-spread-betting.html

You can also open an account with IG Index from this link if you wish. If you do watch this video you will have noted the warning that you can lose money and for this reason it is essential that you read this manual right though before starting trading which fully explains how to manage your risks. However, I have listed the main features of Spread betting below:

1. Profits from financial spread betting are free of tax. This is one of the main attractions for many people. There are no fees or commissions to pay: the only charge is the dealing spread (explained later).

2. You can access thousands of markets from one account. Many Spread Betting companies offer global indices, individual shares, currency pairs, and commodities such as crude oil and precious metals, as well as sectors, bonds, options, binary bets and many more.

3. You can open a trade without putting up the full transaction value; this is known as 'gearing'. For example, if you were to open a trade in Vodafone worth the equivalent of £10,000, you would be asked to initially deposit for just a relatively small amount of this sum. However, you should be aware that this magnified exposure means that you can lose more than your initial deposit – and that's something we need to avoid.

4. You can spread bet whenever and wherever you want. There are no restrictions as to when you can place a bet and many of the markets are available to trade even when the underlying market is closed. Additionally with many companies offering Mobile options to choose from you can access your account whenever you need to, no matter where you are. Your losses can be limited by using Stop Losses with guaranteed stops allowing you to put an absolute limit on your risk without affecting your potential profits.

TERMINOLOGY

Now although my system is extremely simple to use, I want to just go over few things you need to know like some of the terminology, charts details and so on that are used in spread betting first, so that there will be no misunderstanding about the terms I will be using.

Don't worry though; there aren't many of these I want you to know. The last thing I want is for you to become bogged down in a mass of trading terms. All you will be needing is your eyes because my system is totally visual – hence the name **VISUAL FOREX TRADER.**

Two terms that will come across frequently are **bullish** which means the market or prices are going up and **bearish** which means they are going down.

Two more terms you will come across frequently are **going long** or a holding a **long position**. Both of these mean that you are buying. In other words you are expecting the price (or exchange rate) to go up. Conversely **going short** or holding a **short position** means you are selling on the basis that you are expecting the price (or exchange rate) to go down. Explanations for other terms will be introduced as we ago long.

CHARTS

Now I want to discuss the charts we will be using as these will be your main visual trading tools. The first one we will be looking at the Euro/US Dollar which is shown below in Fig 1. This type of chart is what is called a Candlestick Chart because it consists of a series of rectangular bars with spikes or wicks at each end resembling a candle.

The green (or blue) candles indicate that the price is rising and the red ones that the price is dropping. The time is displayed horizontally and the price vertically. You can choose the colour of the candlesticks but usually green or blue are used for rising prices and red ones for falling prices.

Price

Time

Fig 1. Euro/USD Chart

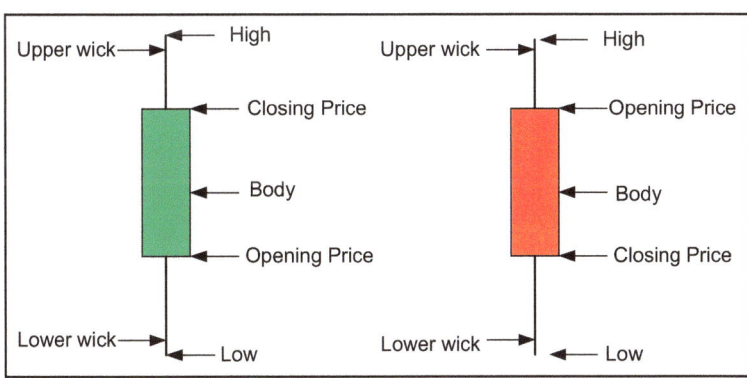

Fig 2 Candlesticks

5

Candlesticks charts can be used over any time scale which may be selected from the chart options. You can choose 1 minute, five minutes, fifteen minutes, 30 minutes, one hour and so on up to a week and a year depending what you prefer. The time interval you select will also determine how long an individual candle is displayed for. E.g. On a thirty minute chart the candle will be displayed for thirty minutes before a new one appears.

As shown in Fig 2, if the closing price is **higher** than the opening price then a green candlestick will be displayed. Conversely, if the closing price is **lower** that the opening price, a red candlestick will be shown. The current position is always shown at the right hand end of the chart.

The coloured part of the candle is known as the body and the thin lines at the top and bottom of the body are known as wicks or spikes. These show the highest and lowest prices that have been reached during the time interval you have selected for your chart. If you hover your mouse over the candle body as shown in Fig 3 below you will see some information displayed showing the opening, closing, highest and lowest prices.

Fig 3 Hovering the mouse for price information

As the price increases, so will the height of the body of the (green) candle and conversely as the price falls the body of the red candle will increase its length in a downwards direction. Long candles reflect strong buying and selling pressure while short candles little buying activity. The current price is always shown at the top of a green (or blue) candle and at the bottom of a red candle.

As you can see from Fig 1 the price fluctuates up and down and the intention of the trader is to buy if he thinks the price is going to go up or sell if he thinks the price will be going down.

Now there are several patterns that traders look for when trading with exotic names like Spinning Tops, Dojis, Marubozu, Inverted Hammer, Hanging Man, Shooting Stars, Bullish and Bearish, Engulfing Patterns, Tweezer Tops and Bottoms, Morning and Evening Stars, Three Black Crows and Three White Soldiers, Three Inside Up and Down and so on!

Apart from these there are almost endless analyses that are performed and in the end traders can often suffer from the well known phrase Paralysis by Analysis!

Don't worry! We do not have to know any of these because the way in which the prices move are almost unpredictable anyway and the reason why so many people lose money when trading. Our approach will be based on carefully studying the graphs and reacting to what is actually happening. This system is *visually reactive* rather than *theoretically predictive*. We will be relying on real time visual signals rather than taking into account the state of the US economy and similar factors that can affect market trading (which, of course, they do). For a long time I got bogged down listening to announcements that might have some bearing on whether the market would be going up or down until I reached saturation point and hadn't got a clue about how to proceed:

After a lot of experimentation and trial and error, I decided I didn't like or want any more of these types of analyses and started to look much more closely at what the charts were telling me instead.

But before I explain my method to you I want to tell you how to set up your charts. First you will need to select a spread betting company and open an account with them. This is quite straightforward and takes only a few minutes.

The company I am using at the moment is IG Index and the charts I am showing are based on their free charting service (once you have opened an account.) There are, of course, many other spread betting companies that you can choose from.

There are also Charting companies that will allow you to use their charts free of charge and one of the best ones is Daily FX. The link to this site is shown below

http://www.dailyfx.com/charts/forexpowerchart/

And I have included a screen capture of the charts they provide below. You will need Java to be installed on your system to be able to see any of the charts and if you do not have it, it can be downloaded from Sun Microsystems at:

http://www.java.com/en/

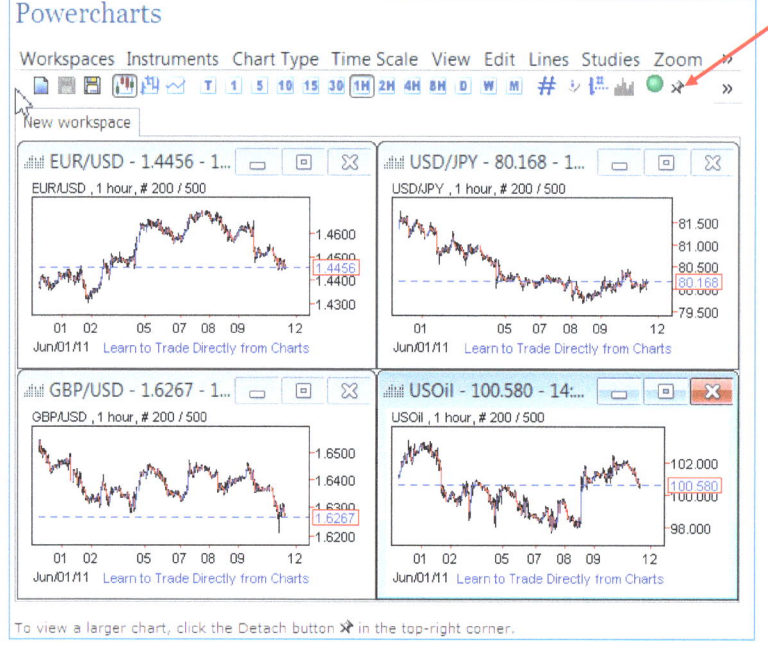

Fig 4 Daily FX Charts

Fig 5 The IG Index Opening Screen

When the charts appear you will see that there are a group of four and they each show a different **instrument**. This simply means EUR/USD; GBP/USD etc. If you want to change an instrument, click on any graph and then click on **instruments** on the top menu bar to choose the instrument you want. Make sure also that you select candlestick from the **Chart type** drop down list.

Once you have done this Click on the **pin button** at the right hand end of the menu bar (which I have marked with a red arrow) to detach the chart and to maximise it to full screen size. Once you have done this you can choose all your preferences from the menu bar.

SETTING UP YOUR CHART

Ok. I will now describe how you should set up your chart based on the free charts that IG Index supply. It is important to do this **before** you attempt any trading because the signals to trade depend completely on the chart settings.

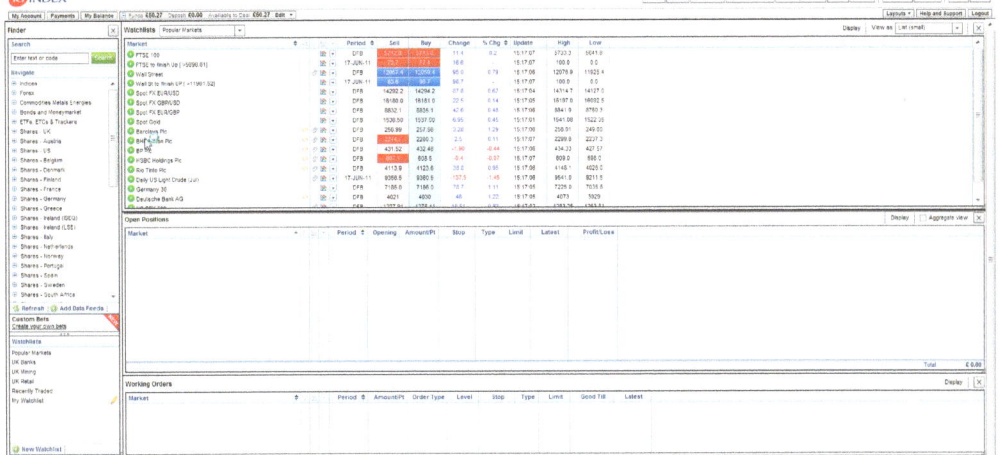

Let's assume that you are going to trade the EURO/USD. The first thing you will see after logging into your IG account is the screen shown below:

As you will see, you are presented with a welter of information which can seem bit daunting at first but once you get used to it, it is quite straightforward.

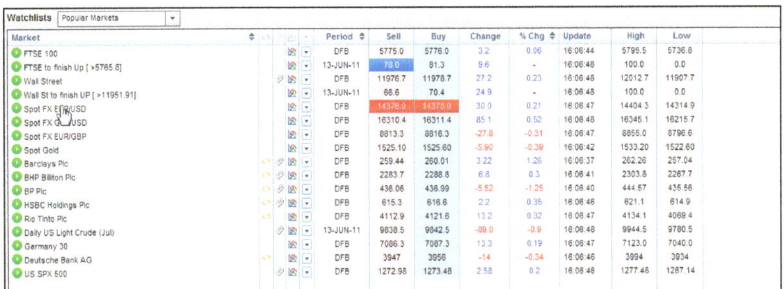

Fig 6 The main watchlist pane

The main pane in the centre of the screen opens with a list of all the most popular markets based on what most people like to trade. However, it is much better to establish you own *watchlist* based on your own personal preferences. It will contain fewer items, be more controllable and you will make fewer mistakes. To start with I will recommend a few of the markets that I trade in order to get you going. These markets are:

FTSE	The main UK Index (Top 100 shares)
EU/USD	The Euro against the US Dollar (USD)

9

GBP/USD	The British pound against the USD
Wall Street	or The Dow Index (main USA Index)
GBP/USD	The British pound against the USD
USD/ JPN	The USD against the Japanese Yen
Silver	
Gold	
GBP/JPY	The British pound against the Yen
GPB/EU	The British pound against the Euro

Table 1 Main trading instruments

My watchlist is shown in Fig 7 below which shows only the markets I have selected.

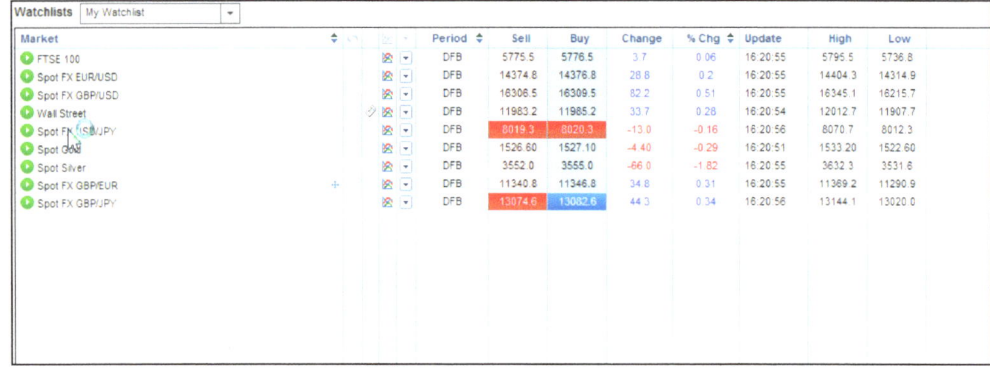

Fig 7. My Watch list

In order to find markets that are not displayed in the popular markets pane, move to the left hand pane as shown in Fig 8.

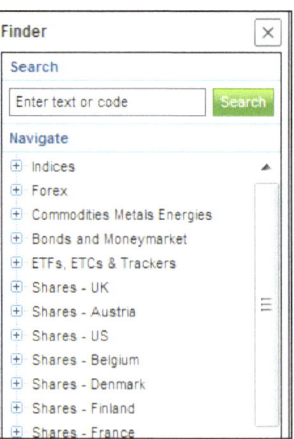

FIG 8 Adding markets to watchlist

Type in the market you are looking for in the search box, click search and keep drilling down until the market appears and click to add to your watchlist. To see the watchlist that you created, click on *My Watchlist* at the bottom of the left hand pane.

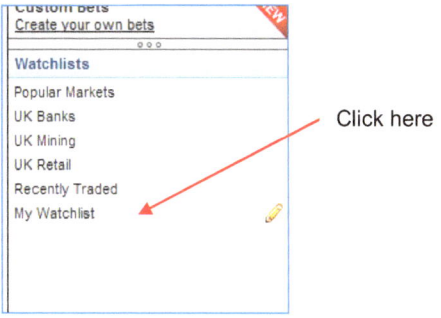

Fig 9 Turning on My Watchlist

OPENING A TRADE

Before you open a trade you will first need to open the chart for the instrument you want to trade. To do this click on the graph symbol marked with a blue arrow in Fig 10. Now open a deal ticket for the same instrument.

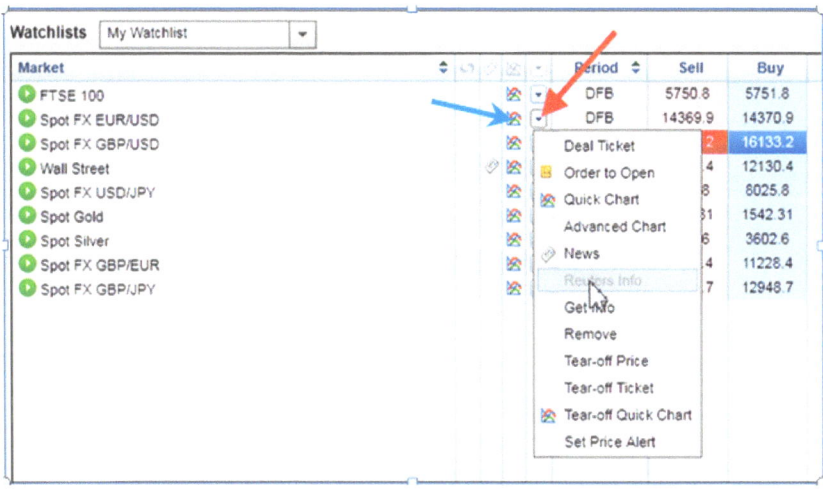

Fig10. Opening a trade from your watchlist – method 1

To do this, click on the small box in line with the instrument you wish to trade – in this case the Euro/Dollar (EUR/USD) and a drop down box appears with a list of options. The second method is to simply click directly on the instrument you want to trade as shown in Fig 11.

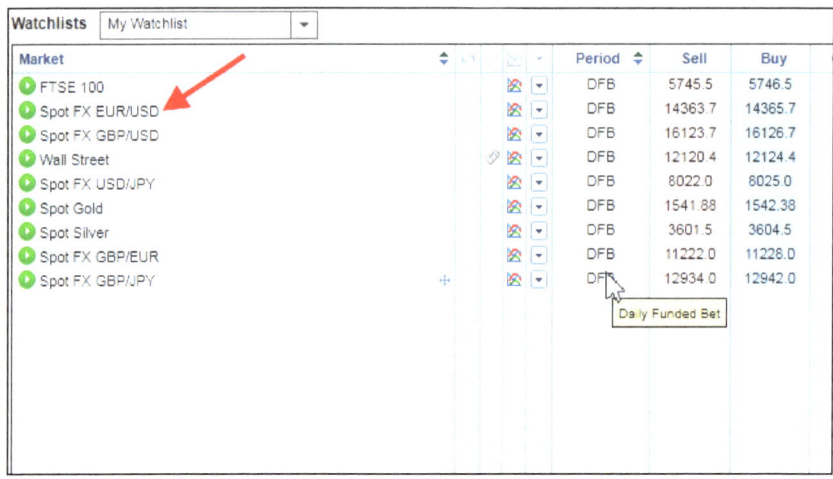

Fig 11, Opening a trade – method 2

In either case, select **Deal Ticket** and this will open in a new window as shown in Fig 12.

Fig 12. Deal Ticket

Enter the amount you want to trade per point or pip in the box marked **size** and also the **Stop Loss** and the **Limit** if any in the appropriate boxes (we will discuss stop losses and limits a little later in more detail).

The next stage is to decide whether you want to buy (because you think the price is going up) or sell (because you think the price is going down). You then click on the Buy or Sell boxes to start the trade.

You will notice that the Buy and Sell boxes show different prices and the difference between them is the **Spread**.

CLOSING A TRADE

When you are trading, the current state of your trades is listed in the open position window. Trades that are in profit are shown in blue and those in a loss situation are shown in red.

Closing a trade is quite straightforward. When your trade moves into a profit and you decide you would like to close the current position, click on the instrument (shown here with a red arrow) on which you are currently trading (the one showing the profit) in the open position window and a new window will open as shown in Fig 13..

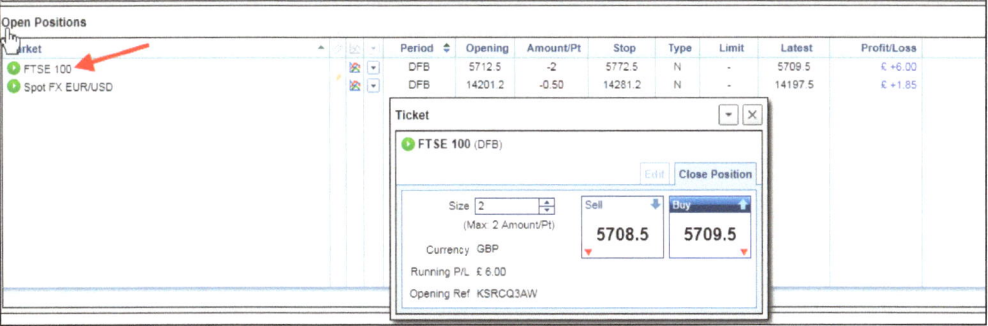

Fig 13. Closing a Trade

Although a buy and sell option will appear, only one of them will be available to close the trade. You can't select the wrong button because only the appropriate button will function. If you have been buying, click the **sell** button. If you have been selling then click the **buy** button. In Fig 13, I am closing the trade on the FTSE which is currently shown in profit.

As soon as you do this, that trade will be closed and it will disappear from your list of open positions. At the same time, the amount of profit you have made will be added to your account balance shown at the top of the screen.

THE SPREAD

The 'spread', also known as the **dealing spread**, is simply the difference between the price at which you can 'buy' and the price at which you can 'sell' a particular market. When opening or closing a bet, you buy at the upper end of the spread and sell at the lower end. For example, if you are being offered the FTSE 100 DFB with IG Index at 5770 / 5771. The spread is one point: if you want to 'buy' you do so at 5771 and if you want to 'sell' you do so at 5770.

This is how the Spread Betting companies make their money and you can immediately see the effect of the spread at work whenever you open a trade. As soon as you click on buy, or sell, you will usually see that you are in a loss situation straight away. This is the amount of the spread that is being charged when you open the trade. The spread varies according to which instrument you are trading but most of the popular markets have a spread of one to three pips.

THE TREND

The first rule of trading (and the most important) is to trade with the trend. The trend is the direction in which the price is going so if the price is rising, the trend is upwards and conversely, if the price is falling, the trend is downward. A downward trend is shown by the blue arrow in Fig 14 below.

Fig 14.The trend based on a one hour interval (Euro/USD)

This shows a graph of the Euro/USD and the current trend is marked by the blue arrow. This clearly shows that the current trend is downwards. However, this is not the complete story. This chart is based is based on a one hour interval but if we switch to a longer time interval – say, weekly, we can see that the underlying trend had been upward as shown in Fig 15. In both cases the trend is indicted by a blue arrow.

Fig 15 The trend based on a one week interval

This shows that the trend over this longer time interval is an upward one. So what does this confusing information mean and how can we make use of it? The Visual Forex Trader is based on what is called *Intraday Trading* where we will be making use of one hourly or thirty minute charts. We will be interested in daily trading where local or current trends like the one shown in Fig 14.

If we were interested in longer term trading, we may well look at a longer term trend like the one shown in Fig 15 and buy on the dips as indicated by the orange arrows shown in Fig 16.

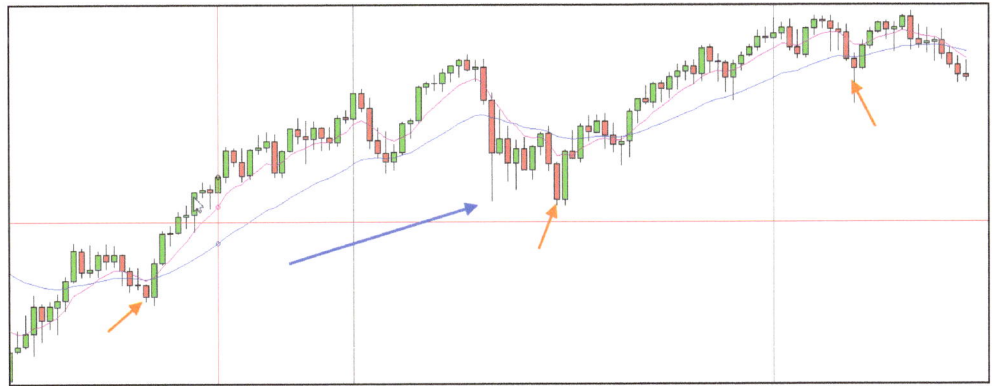

Fig 16. Buying on dips over a longer period of time (Euro/USD)

In each case you can see that if you wait until a dip occurs, like the ones shown, you would buy on the basis that the upward trend would continue and therefore make you a profit. Obviously if the trend was downwards you would wait until a peak occurred and sell as shown in Fig 17.

Fig 17 Selling on peaks over a longer period of time (FTSE)

In this case the trend is downwards as indicated by the blue arrow and the selling peaks are indicted by the orange arrows. You can see in each case a considerable profit could be made from this strategy and many traders use this method very successfully.

There is nothing stopping you trading in this way if you wish but usually this type of trading takes longer to show a profit. For example this graph covers a four day period. However, when your funds increase sufficiently and as you gain in confidence you may wish to try this method. In fact I use this method periodically.

INTRADAY TRADING

Intraday trading as the name implies is a method of trading used to capitalise on very short term movements in price, both long and short (buying and selling).

Most traders are not concerned too much about the fundamental characteristics such as economic or political events, the profitability of a firm or its price/earnings ratio and other socio-economic events.

However, there are a significant number of traders that will trade on information based on these factors, although it is normally a less predictable and less exact method of trading.

A growing number of traders are also using technical analysis or charting, to pinpoint specific levels to enter and exit trades. There are literally hundreds of different technical indicators available for use and probably an equal number of trading systems to go with them, so choosing how to trade and on what basis becomes the real crux of the matter.

Visual Forex Trader is based on Intraday Trading and is designed so that all your trading is normally over in one day.

Having introduced you to the concept of trading, the terms used and the charts, we are now in a position to discuss the details of the Visual Forex Trading System. It is extremely simple and you will have no difficulty whatsoever in using it as it does not require on anything other than recognising certain signals on the charts I have previously described.

THE VISUAL FOREX TRADER SYSTEM

As mentioned previously, there are hundreds of *indicators* that have been devised to tell you when the conditions are right to make a trade. Some of these are quite useful while others are confusing and dubious sometimes giving false signals.

The Visual Trader uses two of these indicators only:

The Exponential Moving Average (EMA)

The Moving Average Convergent/Divergent (MACD)

Don't get thrown by these Flowery titles. I will describe what they mean for the sake of completeness and for those that may like to know but you don't have to know what they mean – you will simply be using them.

The Exponential Moving Average (EMA)

A simple moving average is an indicator often used in technical analysis showing the average value of a security's price over a set period. Moving averages are generally used to measure momentum and define areas of possible *support* and *resistance*.

Moving averages are used to emphasize the direction of a trend and to smooth out price and volume fluctuations, or "noise", that can confuse interpretation.

A basic Moving Average is calculated by taking the arithmetic mean of a given set of values. For example, to calculate a basic 10-day moving average you would add up the closing prices from the past 10 days (shown in red) and then divide the result by 10. In Table 2, the sum of the prices for the past 10 days (120) is divided by the number of days (10) to arrive at the 10-day average. If a trader wishes to see a 20-day average instead, the same type of calculation would be made, but it would include the prices over the past 20 days. The resulting average below (12) takes into account the past 10 data points in order to give traders an idea of how an asset is priced relative to the past 10 days.

	Day 1	Day 2	Day 3	Day 4	Day 5	Day 6	Day 7	Day 8	Day 9	Day10
9	14	12	10	13	11	10	14	15	8	13

Table 2. First ten day moving average

$$(14+12+10+13+11+10+14+15+8+13 =120)/10=12$$

At the end of the next day, the closing price is added to the list and again the last ten values only are added together and divided by 10 to arrive at the latest moving average as shown in Table 2

		Day 1	Day 2	Day 3	Day 4	Day 5	Day 6	Day 7	Day 8	Day 9	Day10
9	14	12	10	13	11	10	14	15	8	13	19

Table 3. Second ten day moving average

This time the last ten days data adds up to 125 and diving this by 10 the moving average for this period is 12.5

The Exponential Moving Average is a modification to the moving average that is similar to a simple moving average, except that more weight is given to the most recent data. The exponential moving average is also known as an **exponentially weighted moving average.**

However, in our case we will be using two EMA's as signals for trading:

The 26 day EMA and the 12 day EMA as shown in Fig 18

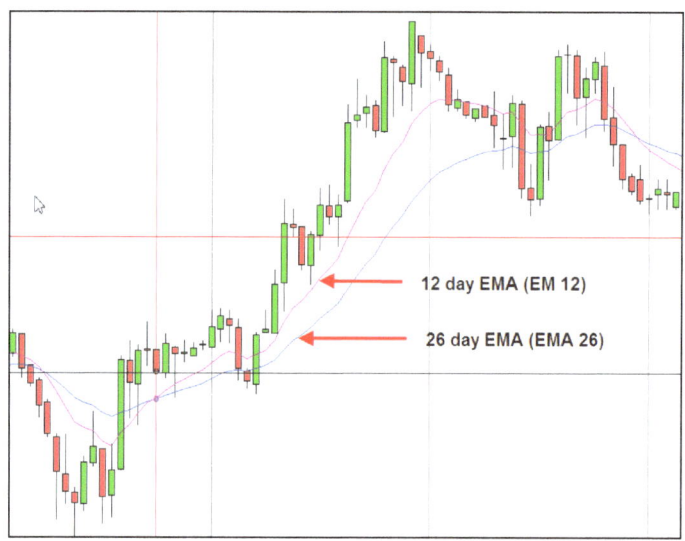

Fig 18. 12 and 26 day EMA lines

The Moving Average Convergent/Divergent (MACD)

This is a trend-following momentum indicator that shows the relationship between two moving averages of prices. The MACD is calculated by subtracting the 26 -

day exponential moving average (EMA) from the 12-day EMA. A nine-day EMA of the MACD, called the **signal line**, is then plotted on top of the MACD, functioning as a trigger for buying and selling signals.

An examples of this is shown below in Fig 19

Fig 19 The MACD Indicator

In Fig 19 when the MACD falls below the signal line (marked as zero and indicated by the blue arrow), it is a **bearish** signal, which indicates that it may be time to sell. Conversely, when the MACD rises above the signal line, the indicator gives a **bullish** signal, which suggests that the price is likely to experience upward momentum.

Many traders wait for a confirmed cross between the two line above or below the signal line before entering into a position to avoid getting into a position too early.

Divergence is when the price diverges from the MACD. It signals the end of the current trend.

A Dramatic rise occurs when the MACD rises dramatically - that is, the shorter moving average pulls away from the longer-term moving average - it is a signal that the security is overbought and will soon return to normal levels.

Traders also watch for a move above or below the zero line because this signals the position of the short-term average relative to the long-term average. When the MACD is above zero, the short-term average is above the long-term average, which signals upward momentum. The opposite is true when the MACD is below zero. As you can see from the chart above, the zero line often acts as an area of support and resistance for the indicator.

In Fig 19 whenever a crossover of the two lines occurs, it is a strong indicator of a buy or sell signal shown by the red arrows. At **A** the two lines are moving downward indicating selling. At **B** there is an upward cross indicating a buying signal and at C there is another downward crossover indicating a selling signal.

Some people find it more useful to display the MACD in different way as shown Fig 20 below:

Fig 20 with bar (or histogram) display

This display is felt to have more visual impact and to be easier to read by many people. It shows the same information as that shown in Fig 19 only in bar form. The green bars indicate upward movement and the red ones downward movement.

Ok, just two more things we need to discuss before we get to the nitty gritty **Support** and **Resistance,** then you will be all set to start making some money.

Fig 21 Support and Resistance

The upper red dotted marks a position where the price has difficulty in breaking through to continue upward. It acts like an invisible barrier preventing the price rising higher. This invisible barrier is known as **Resistance**.

Conversely, the blue dotted line shows a position below which the price cannot break through and fall lower. This barrier is known as **Support**.

We are now ready to look at how we start trading with the **Visual Forex Trader**. Take a look at Fig 22.

I have marked the buying signal in green and the selling signals in red. At position **A** there has been a crossover. It is difficult to see but the lines have actually crossed over twice in a very short distance and as a result the price has moved up over 100 pips.

Fig 22 Trading signals from MACD

In this chart, there is an upward crossover (position **A**) generating a buy signal and as you can see the price has moved up sharply and continues to do so between positions **A** and **B**)

At position **B** there is another crossover, this time a downward one giving a sell signal and the price moves down until another crossover occurs at position **C** when another buy signal occurs. Now this buy signal continues for some time and there are no more crossovers until position **D** is reached.

At position **D** there is a distinct downward crossover indicating a sell signal. This continues until we reach position **F**. This indicates the blip that is occurring with the price rising momentarily and then continuing on its downward movement until Position **E** is reached where a distinct upward crossover occurs giving a strong buy signal.

Al though we will discuss some more tweaks and refinements to this system in a moment you can already see that if you had been buying and selling according to these signal you could have profited from about 200 pips.

Now if you multiply this by this by the stake you used you could have made £400 at £2 per pip and around £1,000 for a £5 stake. Not bad for a single days trading!

Ok. So let's take a look the same chart but this time with the MACD in bar (or histogram) format. This is shown in Fig 23.

Fig 23 Using MACD indicator bars

Here I have marked the chart with arrows. Blue for a buy signal and red for a sell signal.

Can you see what is happening here? In each case the bars form a sort of triangle and in general as the bars slope upwards, the price goes upwards and conversely, as the bars slope downwards, the price goes downwards. At the apex of each triangle, the slope changes indicating a change in the direction of the price.

Yes, there are some fluctuations but overall, this is an excellent indicator telling you **in advance** of what the price is going to do!

In other words, when an apex appears, there will be a change in price direction. I have picked out a couple of examples for you to study in Fig 24 and 25.

Fig 24 Example 1

Fig 24 clearly shows the relationship between the behaviour of the MACD and the effect on the price.

I have included Fig 25 as an example of an apparent anomaly at the position marked **X**. At first sight it may appear that the system isn't working but if you look carefully, you can see that it registered a short upward movement of price and then plummeted downwards again.

You can see from the chart also that the bars, although initially signalling an upward movement, failed to cross the Zero signal line and immediately went downwards again.

You must always be on the lookout for this type of behaviour and as soon as you see it happen, quickly get out of the upward trade you started and sell (in this case) instead.

Fig 25 Example 2

This system is quite sensitive and will pick up short term changes in direction and in this case you could have picked up 20 pips from this movement alone.

Now take a look at Fig 26. What has gone wrong here? Surely the indication is that the price is going up so why is it moving down (indicated by the red candlestick) what's gone wrong? Well actually nothing. There is always some fluctuation of price occurring whether the price is trending up or down.

We do not know yet whether the price will go up or down because we do not have a MACD bar showing another movement. There are two choices in this case. You can either close the trade (assuming you were buying) and get out or wait until you see the next bar appear. The only downside of this strategy is that it will take up to an hour for you to be able to tell (because in this instance we are using hourly charts.)

However, there is one way we can get an indication quite quickly and that is to switch to a 5 minute chart and see what that tells us. We can see the answer in Fig 27. It is still going up after an initial downward movement.

Fig 26 11 hour Euro/USD chart

Fig 27 5 minute Euro/USD chart

Fig 28. Euro/USD still going up

Switching back to the 1 hour chart a short time later we can indeed see that the price is still rising.

Ok. Why not use the 5 minute chart all the time? The reason is that it fluctuates too much and doesn't lend itself to to a sufficeintly stable poistion to obatin meaningful results for the MACD.

Now I now want to introduce you another signal indicator to supplement the MACD. If we draw two moving average lines on our chart it can give use some extra useful information. Looks at Fig 29 below. I have plotted two moving average indicators on this chart (FTSE 1 hour) and I have marked the vertices of the pink line with blue arrows.

Note that every time a vertex (trough and peak) appears that the direction changes. So this is another indicator to add to your armoury.

Fig 29 Vertices on FTSE 1 hour chart

Finally, My last indicator is shown in Fig 30. When a red candlestick crosses the lower line it is a selling signal (shown with red arrow) and when a green candlestick crosses the upper line it is a buy signal (shown with blue arrow).

Ok. Well this is the system but in order for you to start trading, I need to give you a few details on customising your charts, setting stop losses and trailng stop losses and so on.

Fig 30 Using the EMA's for signals

The following charts are all based on the IG Index free charts

Customising your charts

1. Choose an instrument to trade. I would recommend the Euro/USD to start off with.It is not too volatile and you can trade from a 50p stake.

2. Open a chart for this instrument as shown earlier

3. At the top left hand side of your chart there is a menu bar. Click on *indicators* and then click the MA and MACD boxes and enter figures as shown in Fig 31a and 31b respectively

4. Click the *Settings* tab on the menu bar and click the **save as** template option and give the chart a name (e,g. EUR/USD) and click the two option boxes and save your settings for future use.

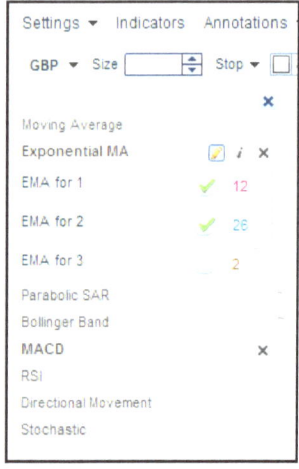

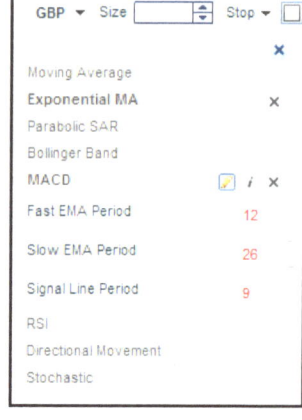

Fig 31a Settings for the EMA   Fig 31b Settings for the MACD

STARTING TO TRADE

1. Now open a deal ticket by clicking on the Euro/USD tab and enter the details as shown in Fig 32.

2. Enter a stop loss figure. I would sugget 60 pips to start with. Stop losses are necessary in order to make sure that you don't not lose too much money if the trade goes wrong. If the trade does go in the opposite direction and a loss stars appearing and grows bigger, the stop loss will be triggered when this figure is reached and your trade will automatically be closed. This amount will be deducted from your acount balance.

3. Enter a limit as shown. This is good practice because quite often a trade will "spike" and trip this figure for you before it reverses direction. If the trade still continues in the original direction you can still go in again. It is also a safeguard in case your computer crashes so that will take a profit while the computer is down if the price reaches the figure you have set.

4. At the bottom of the ticket you will also see the minimum deposit for the trade. It follows therefore that you must have at least this amount of money in your account to be able to trade.

5. Look at your indicators and decide whether to buy or sell and click the appropriate button as shown in Fig 32.

6. As soon as you do this, you will see your trade appear in the *Open Positions* window shown in Fig 33. In this example you can see that I am in a loss situation for the FTSE and a small profit situation for the Euro/UD.

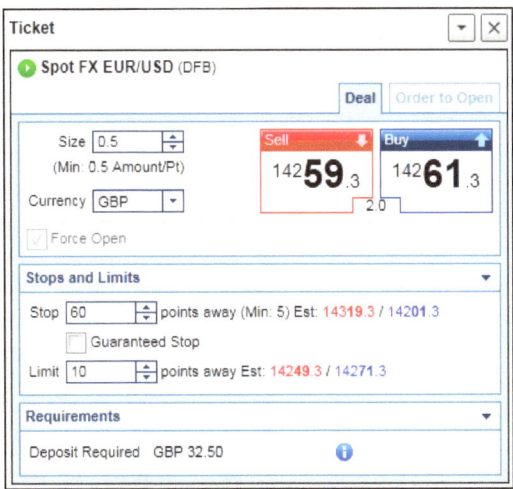

Fig 32 Opening a deal ticket

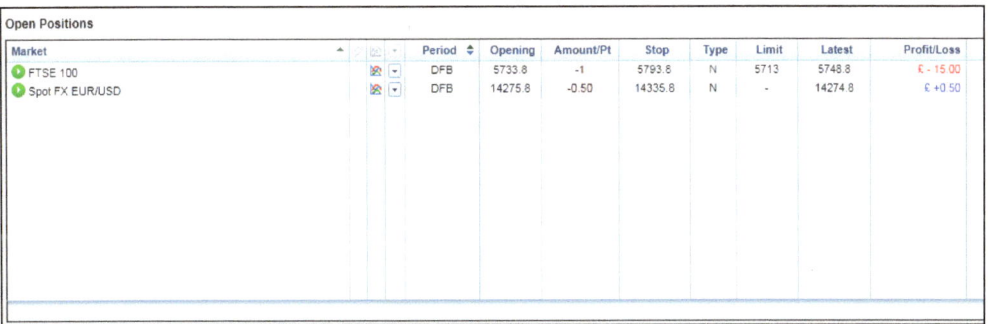

Fig 33 Open positions window

WHAT SHOULD I TRADE

There are literally hundreds of instruments to trade and they can be sub-divided into 5 main groups or types of instruments:

Indices

Sectors

Stocks

Forex

Bonds

Apart from all these, there is an increase in the number of spread betting companies offering to cover any type of bet you like to name. Just one example is that you can bet on the FTSE closing up or down on the opening price sometimes referred to as **CFD's** (contract for difference) bets. Since in this case there are only two possible outcomes your chances of winning this type of bet is 50% or 1 chance in two. So unless you have access to privileged information, you are only likely to break even at best. In my opinion, these types of bets are best avoided for the time being.

For the purposes of this manual we are going to concentrate on just two instruments - Indices and Forex.

INDICES

Again there are many of these to choose from including the French CAC and the German DAX but here we will examine just two – The British FTSE and the American Wall Street.

THE FTSE

The FTSE consists of the top 100 shares of British companies

FTSE operates the well known FTSE 100 Index and FTSE 250 Index as well as over 100,000 other indices, including 600 real-time indices. There are currently seven main groups of indices: Global Equity, Regional and Partner, Fixed Income, Real Estate, Alternative Investment, Responsible Investment, and Investment Strategy. Fees from the use of index information and associated services generate revenues necessary to continue operations. FTSE has offices in London, New York, Paris and other major European and international offices.

The index is maintained by the FTSE Group, an independent company which originated as a joint venture between the **Financial Times** and the **London Stock Exchange**. It is calculated in *real time* (as it happens) and published every 15 seconds.

By far the most widely used is the FTSE 100 UK stock market indicator and although there are other related indices like the FTSE 250 index we will concentrate on the FTSE 100 Index

FTSE100

All instruments have two things in common:

1. They all have a trend which can be up, down or neutral.
2. They are all cyclical in nature. The FTSE in no exception and we can see the cyclical nature of this index in Fig 34.

This chart represents a five day period and the obvious question is why then can we not put on a big enough stop loss to cover the maximum vertical fluctuations so that we would never lose a trade.

Well the answer to this is that you could but looking at the chart you can see that if you bought at position **A** then five days later at position **C**, the price is still lower that that at **A**. Hence you would still be waiting for a profit to occur after five days and this takes no account of the trend which in this case in downward.

Also in this example, you would have to use a stop loss of over 140 points to cover the maximum downward swing of the price marked at **B** (including the spikes).

In fact you might have to wait quite a long time for the trend to change in your favour and in some cases, you may need a considerably greater stop loss in order to make sure that you may ultimately stand a chance of making a profit.

Many people recommend using a stop loss of 300 pips or more but this type of trading is normally used for long term position trading where people don't mind having their money tied up for lengthy periods before getting a return (if at all!).

Fig 34 Cyclical Nature of FTSE 100 index

Of course another factor to take into account is that the behaviour of the FSTE is subject to political and economic events and will sometimes fluctuate wildly depending on what has happened.

It is a mammoth task to keep abreast of these events and their likely implications and it is for this reason that the *Visual Forex trader* was conceived. However this should not stop you from being generally aware of the likely effect of say, the economic collapse of Euro zone countries like Ireland and Greece or the effect of the Japanese Tsunami and the resulting nuclear disaster recently. Clearly, in these cases the prices would drop dramatically so it helps to be forewarned when these major events occur.

Now I do not recommend that you start your trading career with the FTSE because the minimum spread is about 1 pip with most companies and a minimum stake of £1, however, IG Spreads also require a 1 pip spread but requires a minimum stake of £2 which I think is a bit too high to begin with.

One word of warning in case you decide to rush off and start trading the FTSE. The FTSE opens at 8:00 am and closes at 4:30 pm (UK time). You can continue to trade the FTSE outside these times using the simulated (theoretical) trading platforms provided by the spread betting companies but be warned that in case they get it wrong they increase the spread from 1 pip to 5 or 6 pips to cover any differences that might occur. So if you trade after 4.30 pm you will have to suffer the consequences of the increased spread which in the case of IG is 6 pips = £12 at the minimum stake of £2.

WALL STREET (OR THE DOW)

Just like the FTSE, the Wall Street index is based on the performance of the top American companies. The one big difference is that Wall Street fluctuates considerably more than the FTSE.

Fig 35 Two day chart for FTSE 100   Fig 36 Two day chart for Wall Street

Fig 35 and 36 show the close correlation between the two instruments but the Wall Street has increased by nearly 200 pips against the FTSE which has increased by about 100 pips.

Steer well clear of trading on Wall Street until you are considerably more experienced or you could lose a lot of money.

FOREX

The Forex (Foreign Exchange market) is by far the biggest market and covers all major currencies. Clearly, in this market you will be trading on the fluctuating exchange rates between currencies.

Now, you often see reference to **Forex pairs** in financial markets. This simply refers to the vast number of pairs of currencies. E.g. Euro/USD, the USD/Japanese yen, the GBP/USD and so on. Hence the GBP/USD is a **Forex pair**.

The Forex pairs that I trade with most are the Euro/USD, GBP/USD and the USD/JPY and all of these have a 50p minimum stake. I recommend that you start with the Euro/USD for five reasons:

1. As already mentioned the minimum spread is 50p
2. The market virtually never closes(apart from weekends)
3. The spread remains the same throughout
4. It fluctuates less wildly than many other currency pairs
5. It is reasonably active most of the time (although it occasionally goes "dead")

Now IG Index refers to their Forex intraday instrument as **Spot** and lists these as **Spot EU/USD DFB** or spot **GBP/USD DFB**.

A **spot foreign exchange** transaction involves the purchase of one currency against the sale of another at an agreed price for delivery on a value date which is usually the trade date plus two working days - the traditional **spot value**. Banks and investment banks quote two-way markets at which they are willing to trade in a market size with pre-approved credit worthy counterparties – in this case approved Spread betting Companies.

The **DFB** means **Daily Funded Bet** and it is an overnight funding charge that is made if your trade carries on overnight.

The following explanation is given by IG Index:

"At 10 pm on 2 March, our FTSE 100 DFB price is 5950-5951, and you have a long (buying) position open at £5 per point.

The funding charge is calculated as follows:

$D = s \times C \times i / 365$

Where:
D = daily interest adjustment
s = size of bet
C = underlying index price at 10pm (London time)
i = applicable annual interest rate

Daily interest adjustment = (£5 x 5950.5 x 3.12%) / 365 = **£2.543**

3.12% is derived from the LIBOR (London Interbank Offered Rate) for sterling (0.62%) + 2.5%.

Note: The formula uses a 365-day divisor for sterling denominated bets and a 360-day divisor for US dollar and euro denominated bets. Positions held over the weekend will be adjusted for three days' financing.

Interest in respect of long positions is debited from a client's account and interest in respect of short positions is either credited or debited from a client's account.

Don't worry about any of this. Normally your trades will be over in a day but just remember that you will attract a small charge if you leave your trade going all through the night (or nights)."

Now, I mentioned earlier there will be a minimum deposit required each time you trade depending on the particular instrument you have chosen. This is displayed at the bottom of the deal ticket (see Fig 32). It is worked out as follows for a ***non guaranteed stop***.

The following formula is taken from the IG site and is used to calculate the deposit requirement on a position that has a Non-Guaranteed Stop:

"[(Amount per point x stop distance from current level)
+ (deposit requirement for no stop x slippage factor %)]
= Non-Guaranteed Stop deposit requirement"

For example, consider buying £10 per point of FTSE DFB 100 at a level of 5020 when you place a Non-Guaranteed Stop 20 points away.

The deposit factor is 30 and the slippage factor is 20%, so using the above formula the deposit is calculated as follows:

[(£10 x 20) + ((£10 x30) x 20%)] = £260"

A ***Non - Guaranteed*** stop means you are not guaranteed that when your stop loss should be triggered that it will close your trade. In the vast majority of cases it will but lets assume you are trading with the spread betting company's simulated trading platform after the market has closed and when it re-opens their simulated price is different to the actual opening price. This is called ***Slippage*** and this amount can be 20 or 30 pips or so.

Hence, in this case, as soon as the market re-opens and assuming slippage had taken place and exceeds your stop loss, you will be stopped out immediately and probably well in excess of the stop loss you set.

On the other hand, if you choose a **Guaranteed Stop Loss** you will be stopped out at the stop loss you set regardless of what happens but there is a small extra charge made if you want to use this option.

Please bear in mind though that slippage does not normally occur during normal trading hours when the market is open as the current price is always being used.

Having explained all this, **don't be put off**. The actual process is quite simple. Just stick to the indicators I have given you and **start with a 50p stake on the EUR/USD** or at the minimum stake available where it is offered for new members.

This way you can dip your toe in the water gently to start off with. Your money will go further and it will give you time to get familiar with the system. In fact if you prefer, you can paper trade to start off with. Just pretend you are trading and make careful notes on what happened.

Some sites like Capital Spreads offer simulated trading where you can trade for free with dummy money to get familiar with the process. IG offer reduced stakes for a period to get used to their system.

EURO/USD

As I have mentioned before, the Euro/USD (or SPOT FX EUR/USD) is cyclical in nature and failing a major economic disaster will oscillate up and down usually following a trend even if it quite small and sometimes difficult to detect.

This oscillation is normally within 400 pips and as mentioned previously you could set a stop loss of this amount in the hope that it will never be triggered but doing this ties up a lot of money and you may have to wait a long time to get it all back.

Such sums of money could be better used by trading other instruments or by increasing your current stake if your trading is under control.

There are certain obvious things to look for when you first open your chart. The first one is where is the current price – is it in the middle or at the top or bottom of an oscillation?

Clearly if it is at the bottom , it gets harder and harder for it to keep going down and shortly it must bottom out as it meets the lower *support* level and starts moving upwards again. Similarly, if the current level is very high, the same reasoning applies – there must come a point when it meets *resistance* and starts moving downwards again.

One analogy is, the current price is attached to a piece of strong elastic and the further it strays from the norm, the harder it becomes to continue moving away from it until ultimately it is pulled back in. Look at any of the charts and you will see that this is the case – this is what gives the charts their cyclical behaviour.

So when you see the current price up very high or very low – be wary because it may not be long before it starts going in the opposite direction again. If in doubt hold off and watch your charts to determine when the activity will change.

Fig 37 EUR/USD Falling

An example of this is shown in Fig 37 (EUR/USD). The price topped out at the red line position and fell to a lower level (blue line). The question is whether it will go up again or continue downwards. So should we get out and close the trade with a possible a loss (because were buying) or hold fast to allow it to recover.

Well, the indicators are still indicating an upward move and the vertex confirms the upward movement. (Fig 38)

Shortly later the price had fallen further – now down 20 pips and nail biting time sets in. should we get out or not? Those indicators are still showing an up so should we believe them. Do you trust your indicators or ate you going to override them?

First of all, there will always be some vertical oscillation as a price moves in either direction as illustrated in Fig 38.

Fig 38 Natural oscillations of EUR/USD

You can clearly see that as the price moved upwards or downwards, there are times when it reverses direction for a short time and then continues in its original direction. This behaviour is common to all instruments and to be expected and is called **retracement.**

The question still remains: how long should we wait before getting out? Experience counts for a lot in these situations but as a rule of thumb I would not let this retracement continue beyond 30 pips.

Look at it this way, you have already lost 30 pips and you no longer have the amount this represents available to trade with. This is reflected by the **Available to Trade** figure (shown next to your **Account Balance)** which will reduce as your loss increases, so you might as well get out and see what happens next, to stop you losing any more in case the price continues to drop even further. Or think of it yet another way. If you closed out your current trade at 30 pips down that would immediately be shown in your account balance. You don't actually have it – it's already gone. The advantage of this technique is that you pause for a moment or two until you are clear on what is happening and then start trading again.

Fig 39 shows a position on the EUR/USD which had been steadily going upwards but then suffered a **retracement** or **reversal**, dropping down quite quickly to the position shown. Once again, the question is whether we should close the trade or let it run on. In this case both the indicators marked in blue were still showing a strong upward signal.

I decided to hang on and see what developed but ready to close the trade if things deteriorated further. Now we will take look at what actually happened. This retracement/ reversal amounted to 23 pips at this point and I held on to see whether I should get out of the trade when it reached 30 pips.

Fig 40 shows the outcome. In this case, after this retracement/ reversal, the price went up again as shown and spiked through the previous high in Fig 40 although this did not happen until quite some time later on. After a short period of stagnation the price continued to climb again. Hence the movement was due to a retracement and not a reversal.

Fig 39 EUR/USD with indicators still showing upward movement

Fig 40

In fact the price continued to climb for some time afterward as shown in Fig 41. You can see the original position marked with a blue dotted line and the current position marked with the red dotted line.

It is at this point that I would begin to look closely at the indicators ready for the price to top out. Why? Because the price has risen to a level near the highest it has reached for several weeks. Remember the EUR/USD like all instruments, is cyclical and at some point it will start to nose dive downwards once again as it always does.

Fig 42 illustrates this very well. Just look at the previous high marked with the red dotted line a week before and the way the price plummeted shortly afterward. The MACD indicator is also not very positive.

Given these factors I would be very hesitant about buying again in this position and would hold off for a while to see how things develop first. I would prefer to see a distinct MACD signal before doing anything.

This is not rocket science it is an obvious cautionary tactic. It does not mean that the price will not rise higher and start a new upward trend but as yet we don't know. And if you are uncertain **you do not trade.**

Fig 41

Fig 42

If I see the upper pink line (MA12) show a downward vertex coupled with a down signal form the MACD. I would immediately sell. So I will have to wait to see for a while.

I am still waiting sometime later but the mere fact that the price had not risen any higher may well mean it has hit a *resistance* level. I will not trade until I know for sure.

Well, I now have the answer, the price has broken through this resistance and is climbing again. The MACD is also showing a stronger buy signal and there is no sign of a downward vertex on the MA 12. By the way I am doing this live at the time of writing so I really am relying on all the signals I have described to you, to know what to do next.

Based on these signals I decided to buy and shortly afterwards I has made another 20 pips profit and the price has now reached the level of the previous weeks high.

A few moments later we can see the price has overtaken the previous weeks high (Fig 43) and I am still buying. However, I am still wary about the possibility of a *rebound* downwards with the price is this high.

Fig 43

GBP/USD

This is another popular instrument to trade and once again you can trade this with a minimum stake of 50p. It has a spread of three pips and can be a little more volatile that the EUR/USD.

Fig 44 EUR/USD

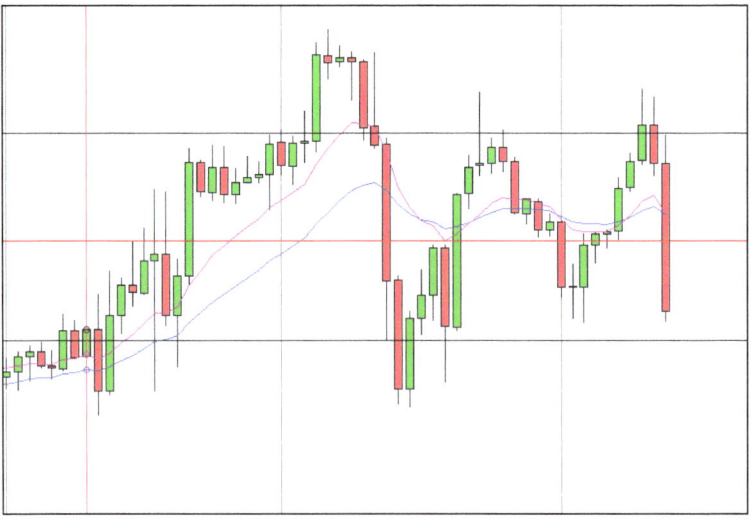

Fig 45 GBP/USD

The reason I do not recommend you starting with the GBP/USD is illustrated tin Figs 44 and 45. They both represent the same time and date and you can see that the GBP/USD is considerably more volatile than the EUR/USD.

Note that two charts are almost the same as each other. When the EUR/USD goes up, the GBP/USD goes up and when the EUR/USD goes down, so does the GBP/USD. The difference being the much greater fluctuations of the latter.

It can move quite rapidly and is probably best left until you have gained familiarity with the system using the EUR/USD first. However, having said that, all the indicators I have already given you will work with this instrument (in fact they will work with all indices and Forex instruments).

SOME DO'S AND DON'T'S

There are some golden rules associated with trading and some other tips and wrinkles I would like to share with you;

- Never trade more than you can afford to lose.

- Always trade with the trend – The trend is your friend.

- Always set a suitable stop loss. This is a must to prevent you losing a lot of money due to a sudden rebound or if your computer decides to crash or "hang up".

- Make a trading plan and stick to it.

- Always set a sensible stop loss and never increase it – don't let emotion rule.

- Do not set optimistic limit orders on your profits 10 to 15 pips is reasonable. 50 is not. Take your 10 to 15 pip profits and get out (close the trade). You never know when there will be reversal. So take the profit while it's there.

- Always set a profit limit. It will catch sudden quick spikes and safeguard if your your computer crashes.

- Always pause after completing your trade to see if you can use a retracement to your advantage.

- Don't get bogged down with too much analysis. Use the indicators I have given you and stay with them.

- Constantly study your charts and gain experience in what they are telling you

- Trade with a small group of instruments and get to know them well.

SUMMARY OF TRADING TECHNIQUES

Ok – here is a quick reference guide to all the techniques I have been discussing so far in this manual.

There are three indicators that we need to use:

The MACD

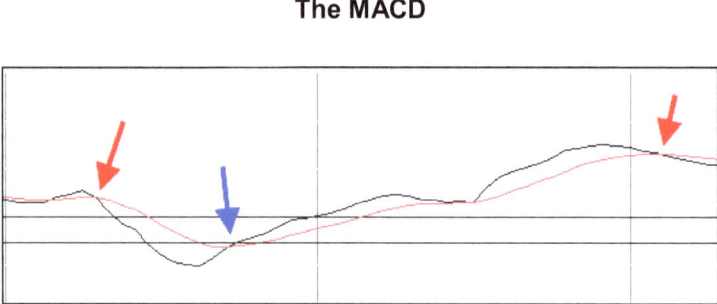

Fig 46 The MACD Indicator (with lines)

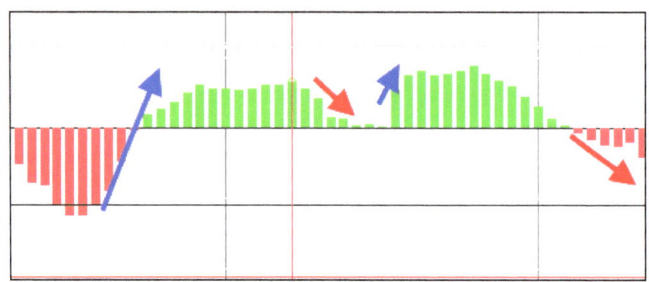

Fig 47 The MACD Indicator (with bars)

The MACD can be displayed in line form or bar (or histogram) form as shown in Figs 46 and 47. Both show the buying and selling signals marked with blue and red arrows respectively here.

The EMA 26 and EMA 12 Vertex Indicators

Fig 48 EMA 26 and EMA 12 Vertex Indicator

The buying signals are again show here with blue for buying and red for selling. The strength of the signals is indicated by the length of the arrows here with three very strong and one weaker selling signal.

The EMA 26 and EMA 12 Crossing Indicators

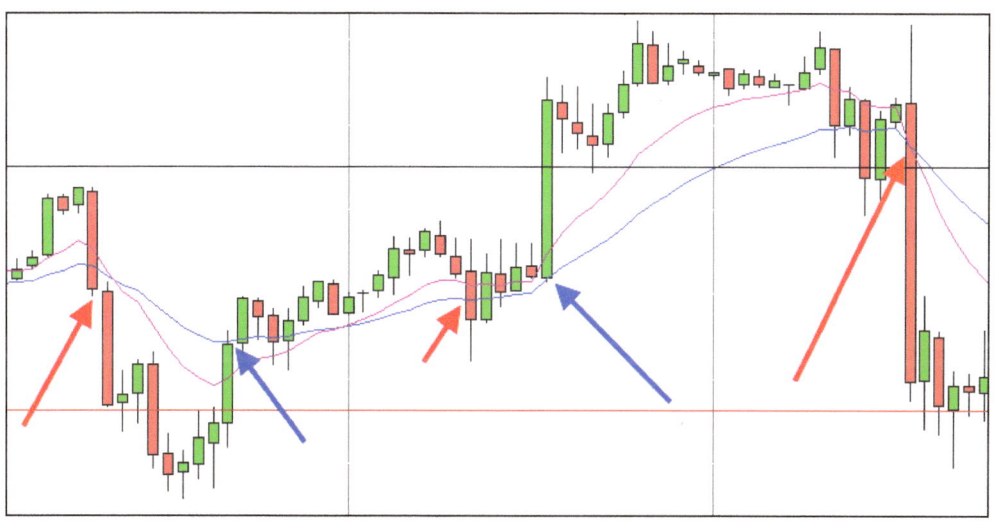

Fig 49 EMA 26 and EMA 12 Crossing Indicators

Again here, the strength of the crossing signal is shown by the length of the arrows.

Fig 50 shows the remarkable agreement of signal of all three indicators. Here they are shown grouped by colour. As you can see, when all three indicators are in agreement agree like this it signals that a considerable movement is going to take place. You can't fail to make significant profits from these situations.

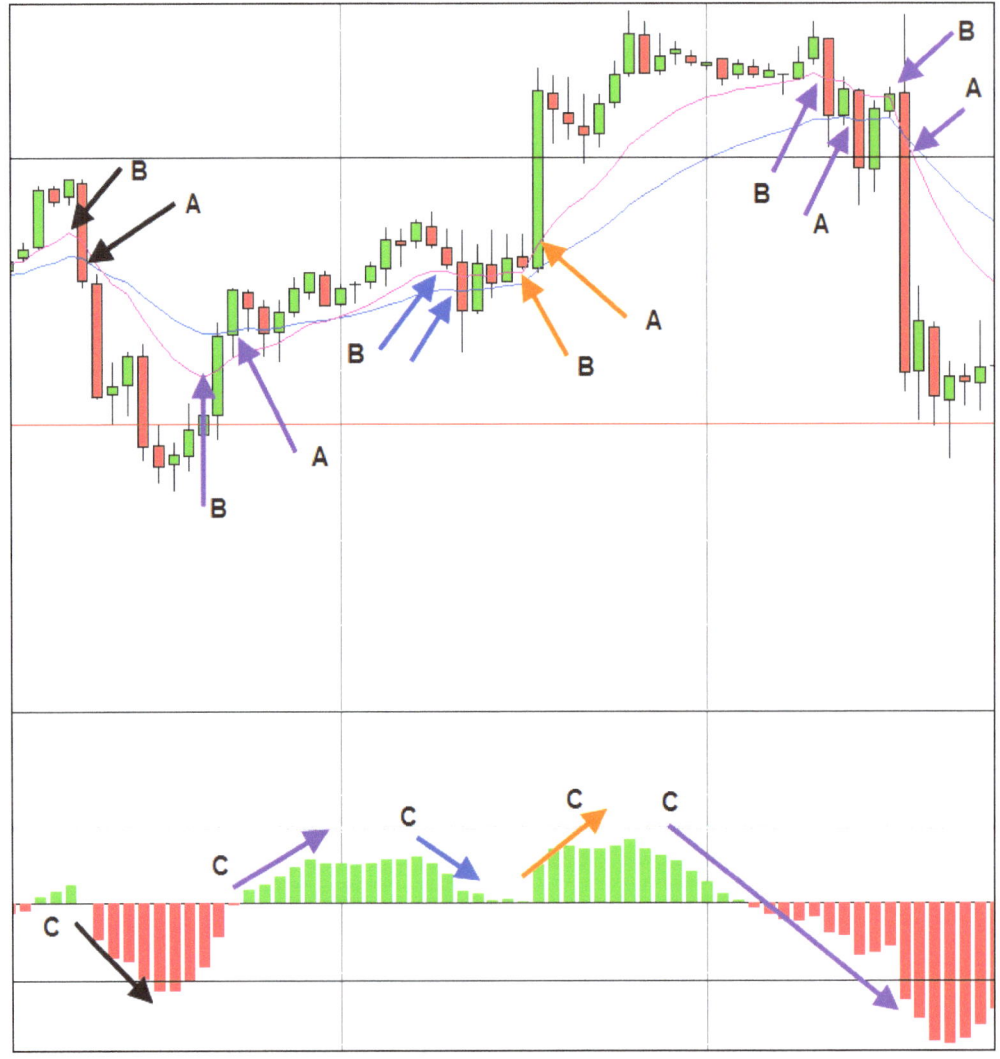

Fig 50 Agreement of all three indicators

In this figure I have marked the indicators as follows:

A EMA Crossover Signal

Fig 51 EMA Crossover Buy Signal   Fig 52 EMA Crossover Sell Signal

B EMA Vertex Signal

Fig 53 Vertex Buy Signal   Fig 54 Vertex Sell Signal

C MACD Signal

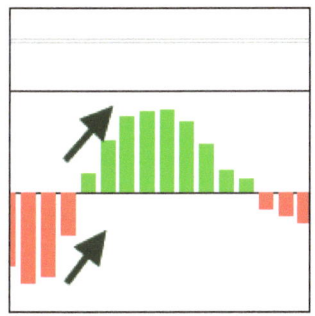

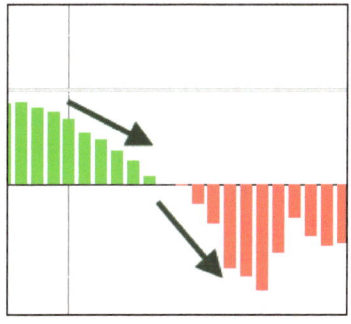

Fig 55 MACD Buy Signal   Fig 56 MACD Sell Signal

Fig 50 looks complicated but in reality, the signals are fairly obvious but shown once again individually in Figs 51 to 56 for clarification.

However you must always keep an eye on your charts to make sure you do not miss any signals especially those that are telling you the price will shortly be going in the opposite direction to one you are trading in.

As you gain more experience you will be able to interpret even small signals that you can take advantage of to make smaller (say 10 pip) profits. All these add up to quite significant amounts and since we are in the business of profit making we don't want to miss out on them.

Be sure you understand what the MACD is telling you. Look at Fig 57 it gives clear advance warning of a change of direction.

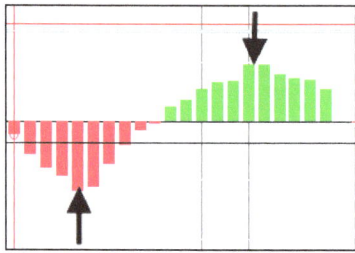

Fig 57 MACD warning signals

The red bars on the left are telling that the price is going down until it reaches a minimum indicated by the black arrow. The bars then start reducing height indicating a change is about to occur and starting to give you a buying signal.

Similarly the green bars are signalling a sell signal once the maximum value had been reached and subsequently they start to reduce in height giving you a sell signal.

Also bear in mind that that when you trade in accordance with these signals, the price will not go steadily continually upwards or downwards. There is a natural tendency for it to oscillate up and down as it follows a particular direction due to *retracement*.

This effect can be seen in Figs 58 to 60 below.

Fig 58

In Fig 58 I am selling as all the indicators have told me to do this and you can see the point that I started the trade shown by the blue arrow and I have drawn a line across on the chart at my entry price as a visual aid for reference which I always do.

You can see that that almost immediately, the price has gone up (the wrong way). However Fig 59 shows the position about a minute later. You can seen that the price has now started to drop down towards my entry level line and finally in Fig 60 you can see the price has now crossed my entry line as is nicely proceeding downwards in the direction I want and of course, into profit.

This is the natural effect of **retracement** described of earlier and fluctuations both up and down are usually bound to occur. The only exception to this is when there has been a **breakout** where the price has suddenly shot up or shot down very rapidly.

Fig 59

Fig 60

This is why it is very important to set a stop loss figure that is great enough to absorb these fluctuations but that will also end your trade if there was a sudden big surge against you.

Remember that no system is perfect and sometimes you will have to accept losses. However, this system will give you the correct indications not less than 80% of the time which should see you handsomely rewarded with substantial profits.

ADVANCED TRADING TECHNIQUES

Take another look at Fig 45 and in particular all those fluctuations up and down. Sometimes, the fluctuations are so quick that they are difficult to keep up with but it would seem a shame not to take advantage of all these movements wouldn't it?

Well the answer is that we can! How? The answer is simple – by buying and selling the same instrument at the same time. Not all Spread Betting companies allow you to do this but some do – like IG Index.

Please do not attempt this method before you have gained a lot of experience trading normally or you could get into difficulties very rapidly.

Very often you do not know whether the price is going to rise or fall and I have already explained that there is a natural oscillation or fluctuation most of the time anyway.

Therefore to take advantage of this you need to open two trades in opposite direction – one buying and one selling. Obviously, if you start by buying, pause for a moment to see if the price is going up and if it is, then delay starting a new selling trade until the upward movement pauses and stutters. When it does, then open a new selling trade.

One of these is bound to show a profit almost immediately. Once this profit starts to stutter, close the position and pause and wait to see what happens before opening another trade.

Let's see how this strategy works. Take a look at Fig 61. It is not clear what is going to happen here. The price is oscillating up and down wildly and we are getting a frequently changing buying and selling signals which are starting to get difficult to keep up with so lets look carefully at the chart to see if we can detect anything to our advantage.

First of all, on this chart, each division represents 10 pips, so that we can see that the total fluctuation takes pace over about a 70 pip cycle. However, in this case, we can also see that this fluctuation (or cycle) looks very much like it is going to be a repetitive one and may continue with this behaviour for some time. This rapid up/down behaviour is reflected by the MACD and the MA indicators which are gyrating all over the place to keep up.

Therefore, if we start a trade at the top (or the bottom) of this cycle, we will be instantly into a profit if we trade in the appropriate direction. Fig 62 focuses on this cyclic behaviour and I have illustrated the cycle with the dotted red lines. You can clearly see from this that if you had started trading at point **A** and followed it through to point G, you would have made a profit of roughly 250 pips. Multiply

Fig 61 Fluctuations on EUR/USD

Now, as soon as this retracement starts to stutter, you close your selling trade and take this profit while your buying position climbs back again past this retracement and continues on its upward journey. The net result is that you will have collected 40 + 25 pips instead of just the 40 pips.

If you look at the chart carefully, you will see that there are retracements both up and down for at least three cycles and on average you can pick up another 50% profit with this technique so your total profit could be around 250 + 125 pips = 275 pips!

Hence if you watch out for this type of behaviour on your chart, you can take maximum advantage of not only the cycle but all of the retracements that take place in it as well. I know this all sound rather complicated but the technique is very simple really. As mentioned previously, there will always be retracements in all cycles and trends. They are a natural occurrence as the prices fluctuate up and down within its general direction.

Always be on the look out for this type of behaviour which occurs quite frequently. Another example of this is shown in Fig 63 below.

Fig 63 Another example of cyclic behaviour

Now a word of warning! There **will** come a point when this cycle will be broken as the price breaks through its local **resistance** or **support** levels, in this case shown by the dotted red lines in Fig 62, and for this reason it is very important that you set adequate stop losses to cover for this.

I cannot stress this point strongly enough and I make no apologies for repeating he reasons for always using stop losses on each and every trade.

1. It will limit any loss to the level you have set to protect you from any sudden, unexpected surges in prices upwards or downwards.
2. If your computer crashes or the spread betting site crashes, it will protect you against potentially very high losses when you get your computer back on line

or the site problems clear. In fact in some cases, it is possible for you to owe the spread betting company money in the event of a dramatic surge against you.

3. Stop losses prevent you losing all the money in your account and wiping you out completely, resulting in you not being able to trade any more until you put more money in your spread betting account.

A practical example of how you can get wiped out without a stop loss being in place is shown below in Fig 49.

In this case the trend has been progressively going steadily upwards with a few retracements on the way as normal. However, in this example, the price reaches point **A** and suddenly drops quickly to point **B** before rapidly recovering again and continuing with its upward trend which represents more that a normal retracement. Now in this case the effect only represents about 70 pips but it can easily be as large as 100 -150 pips or more and can easily wipe you out completely if you haven't set a stop loss – so be warned!

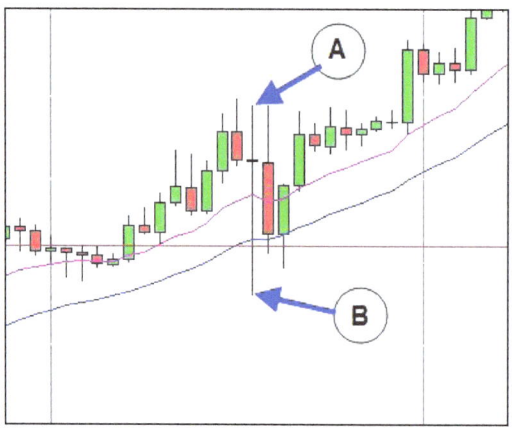

Fig 64 Whipsaw effect

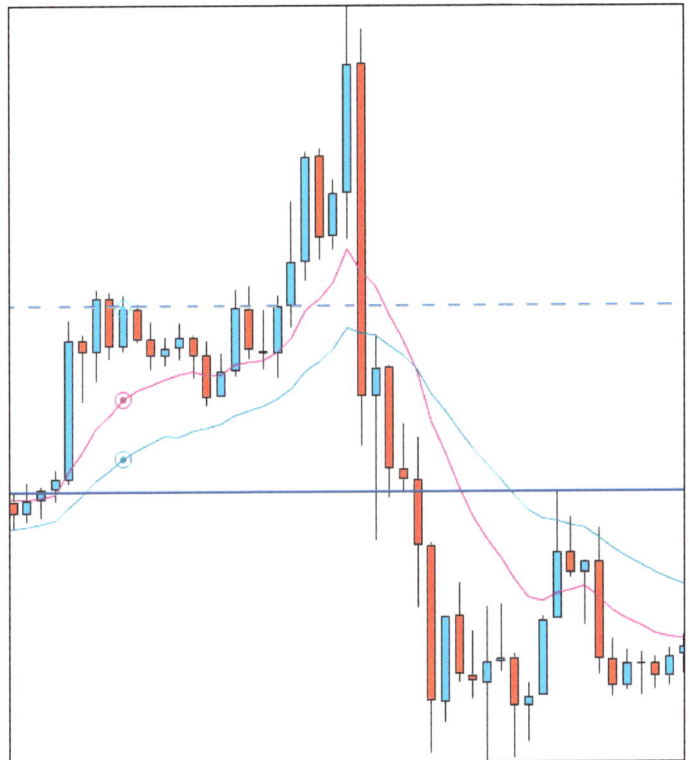

Fog 65 Surge in EUR/USD

Another example of what can happen is shown in Fig 65 where the price has dropped almost 90 pips.

HEDGE BETTING

Whilst you should always be on the lookout for the type of restricted cyclic trading so that you can take advantage of it, you can apply the same technique generally to all your trading.

Lets say you are about to start trading and open up the EUR/USD chart and are presented with the situation shown in Fig 66. Our first job is to look critically at the chart and the indicators to see whether there is anything we can see that we can trade.

Well, in this case the MACD is indicating that the price is rising and we decide to buy at position **A** and indeed we pick up 40 pips fairly quickly. Shortly afterwards, the price starts to stutter and the vertex in the EMA confirms this. So we take the profit and sell at position **B** and pick up another 30 pips as the price drops again. Shortly afterwards the MACD is showing another buy signal and we buy at position **C**. After a bit of dithering, the price rises and continues to increase another 60 pips. So far we have picked up 130 pips and begin to wonder if a cycle is starting.

Fig 66 Opening condition of EUR/USD

Fig 66

A short while later we can see that a cycle is starting a shown in Fig 66.

We now mark in the upper and lower dotted red boundary lines and trade within them using the same technique to enable us to pick up hundreds of pips profit over the next few hours.

However, in order to catch all the retracements that are taking place, we could simply note that the two boundary lines are about 170 pips apart and set a stop loss of 200 pips and then open a buying and selling trade simultaneously.

Clearly one of these will show a profit straight away and using our indicators, we take the profits as they occur and instantly start another new trade in the **same** direction as the one you have just closed. So if you have made a profit buying, you sell and then immediately open another buying trade so that there are always the two opposing trades in force – one buying and one selling.

But you must keep your eyes open to see whether the price is approaching the upper or lower boundary lines. If it does then stop trading in that direction since very soon the price will swing again in the opposite direction. Your open positions window will show some quite large losses whilst trading in this way but as long as the cycle holds each buy and sell trade will cycle through profits and losses alternately until the cycle is broken and you actually lose nothing.

You continue to use exactly the same technique until the price starts to break through the boundary line, indicating that the cycle had ended. If this happens, close the losing trade and take the loss but remember, you will still have the profit making trade open which starts to make another profit as the breakout continues.

Keep consulting your indicators and trade normally with the trend until another cycle appears when you can repeat the same swing trading procedure again.

The only downside of this way of trading is that you may make an actual loss when the cycle ends (due to a breakout) but this will be very small compared with the profits you will have taken while the cycle lasts. Note that you will need a stop loss corresponding to the difference between the red dotted boundary lines plus a buffer amount for each buy and sell trade you make. Hence you will need at least twice this amount in your account balance before you start. In the above example, we have a boundary difference of 170 pips and I have used a stop loss of 200 pips for each trade so that you would need to have provision for covering around 500 pips in your trading account. However, this only amounts to £250 if you trade at 50p per pip.

SERVICES AVAILABLE TO HELP WITH YOUR TRADING

Several spread betting companies offer information services that can provide predictive information on how instruments are likely to behave to assist you with your trading. This information is complied by a team of experts in the analysis and prediction of trading and is usually provided free of charge.

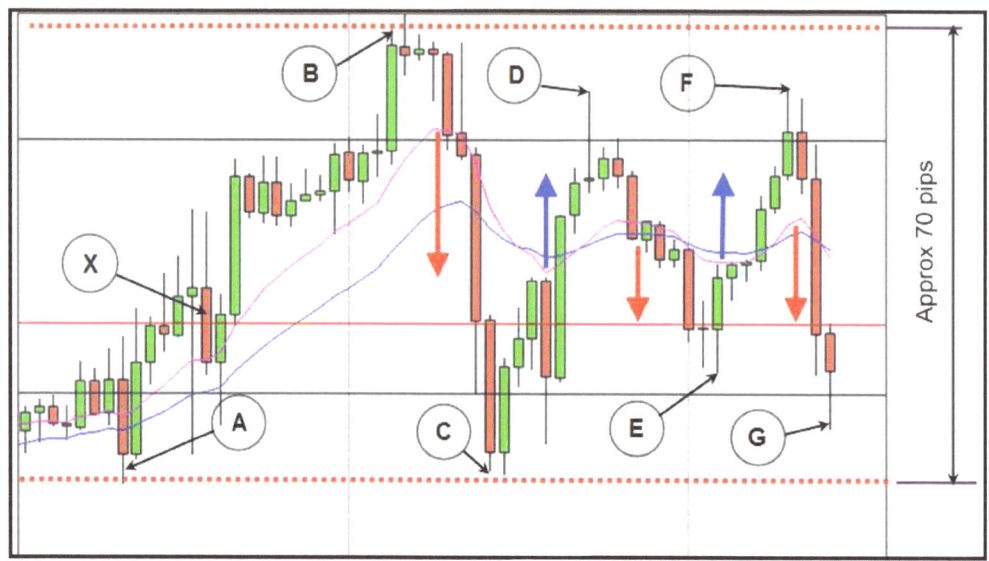

Fig 62 Trading the Cyclic Fluctuation

this by your stake and you can see this represents a large profit - £125 at a 50p stake and £1,250 at a £5 stake and all in a six hour period (30 min chart).

The point I am making here is that if you had been trading in one direction only – as you should have been up to now, you would have lost the profits that you could have made due to the continued cycling behaviour of the price.

I will now illustrate the procedure that is required to take full advantage of this situation. First, refer to Fig 62 and let's say you bought at point A (because the MACD in Fig 62 is showing a buy signal). This decision seems to be the right one as for the next forty minutes the price continues to climb nearly forty pips. However, at this point, a retracement occurs and the price drops back 25 pips.

The MACD shows a slight drop and then recovers, while the EMA hardly responds at all, both indicating this is a temporary blip and that the price is likely to continue to rise. Given this information, we should disregard the blip and resist the temptation to sell. Similar retracement blips occur until the price reaches point **B** where it stutters and because it is now at the upper bound level (the upper dotted red line), we should be prepared for the direction to change and indeed the price starts to fall, which it does all the way down to point **C.**

If you were trading in one direction only, you would miss the profit of 25 pips due to the retracement at position **X.** You would have to wait until had finished and the price started to rise again. On the other hand, if when you saw this retracement start, you had opened another trade in the opposite direction, you would have immediately taken advantage of the profit as well.

The example shown in Fig 67 below is supplied by IG spreads but similar services are available form other companies as well.

At the top right had side of the IG opening page there is a list of tabs available and if you click on 'Tools' a drop down box appears as shown in fig 68

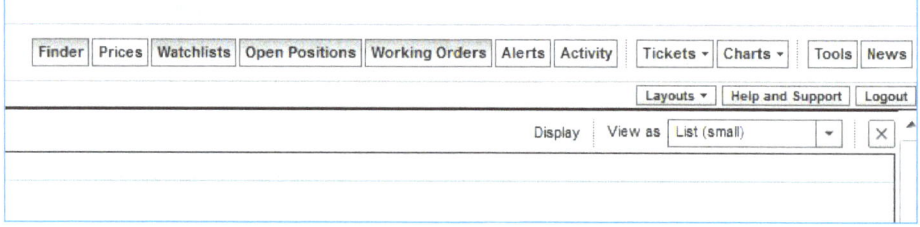

Fig 67 IG Tool and news service tabs

Now click on the tools tab to display another box as shown in Fig 68. This presents you with a whole list of options that you may like to investigate further. The one we are most interested in is the "Trading Central" option and if you click on this, you will be presented with a wealth of information on market analysis as shown in Fig 69. It covers all instruments and gives you their opinion about the way each of them is going to behave.

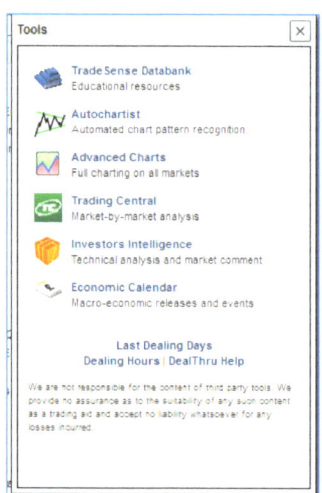

Fig 68 Trading Information

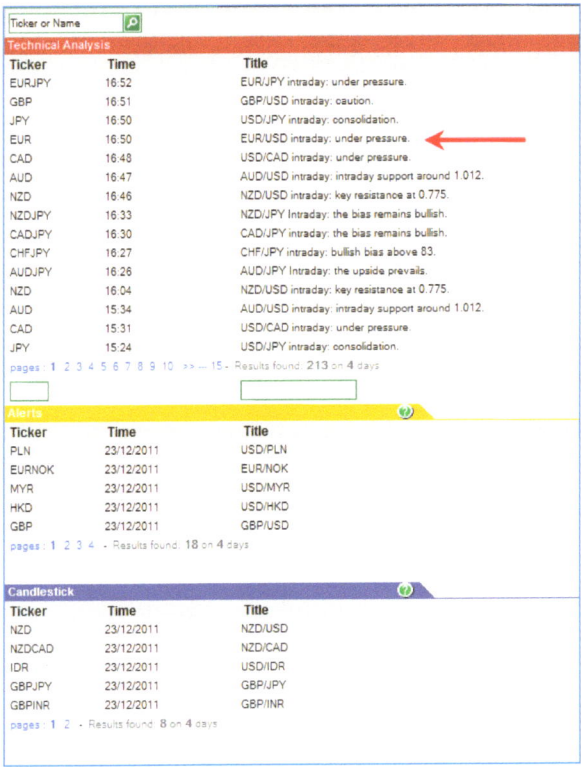

Fig 69

I have marked the option we are interested in with a red arrow – the EUR/USD and if we now click on that we obtain the information shown in Fig 70.

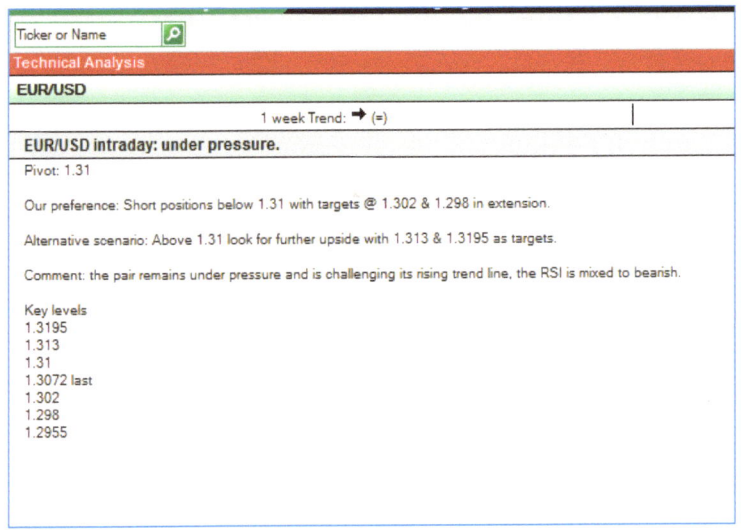

Fig 70 Trading information on EUR/USD

This gives you their opinion on what is likely to happen and is specifically dedicated to **Intraday** trading and this information is updated several times each day. The first thing we should take note of is the **Pivot Point.** A pivot point is a line which predicts whether the price will be below or rise above it depending on the prediction. In other words all the action will take place above or below this line and not cross it.

Am example is shown in the chart shown below (Fig 71).

The information in this example means that in the opinion of Trading Central, the pivot point or line will be at 1.310 and the price will remain below this line with the possibility that it may fall and finish up at 1.302 – 1.298 which is quite a drop in price and is off the bottom of the chart. Note that they also give an alternative scenario if the price rose above the pivot line of 1.313 – 1.3195.

Fig 71. Graph showing pivot point

The reason for this alternative scenario is that they can only predict how the instrument is going to behave within quite a wide range – in this case about 215 pips. Although this does give us some idea, it clearly illustrates just how difficult it is to predict what is going to happen – if a team of trading experts can't get any closer than this, what chance do we lesser mortals have of trying to predict it any better!

It is precisely this notorious difficulty of prediction that made me look for alternative methods of trading and developing the *Visual Forex Trader*. However, the information provided by Trading Central is better that nothing – it gives you some idea rather than none.

Another more useful service offered by Trading central is that they will issue warnings when things are about to change if you select this option. These appear as shown in Fig 72

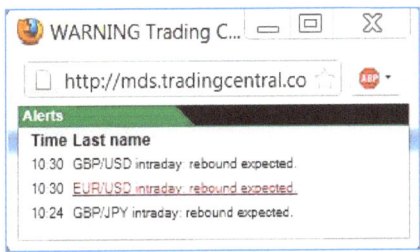

Fig 72, Warnings issued by Trading Central

To enable these on your computer, select the "Portfolio" tab and then click the "customise my access" link at the top of the screen. Then then add your preferred instruments and tick the boxes labelled "I would like to receive alerts by pop ups." You will also have to make sure your browser allows these pop ups though – usually accessed via the tools then options tabs. Or you can click the option that says "Allow pop ups from this site" in this window."

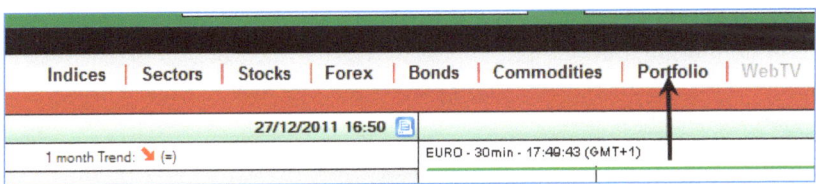

Fig 73 Accessing the portfolio tab

Spread Betting Tutorials

There are a wide range of tutorials available on the internet if you would like some further information. I have selected just three here that are quite good.

http://www.financial-spread-betting.com/spreadbetting-glossary.html

http://www.igindex.co.uk/spread-betting/how-it-works.html?QPID=1143548&QPPID=1&s_kenid=_3abe5e2b-e488-8de9-0b0a-000069d8f6b6_&gclid=CJeog8bqpK0CFYulfAod8UKRng

http://www.independentinvestor.co.uk/spread-betting/glossary.php

The link for another comprehensive one is Financial Betting – a Traders Guide;

http://www.financial-spread-betting.com/academy/trading-course.html

Spread Betting Companies

Again there is a vast range of spread betting companies available to choose from and each of them had advantages and disadvantages. I have listed the three that I use the most but make sure you fully understand the terms and conditions of any offers they are making before you jump in. Most companies offer a bonus after you have deposited a certain amount of money into your trading account and have completed a number of trading transactions. They all offer mobile phone apps so that you can trade on the move.

IG Index: Reduced stakes for beginners, seminars

www.igindex.co.uk

Capital Spreads: £100 credit after qualifying period. Free demo account

www.capitalspreads.com

Finspreads: £100 credit after opening account + a number of trades

www.finspreads.com

During the course of writing this book, IG Spreads launched their own charts which are very similar to the third party ones they used before and they do have one or two useful extra features on them that may need a little explanation.

The general layout of the graph is very similar to the others we have been looking at throughout the manual but one useful addition to the new charts is that you can now trade directly from the chart itself. Fig 74 shows the new interface for doing this which is quite straightforward.

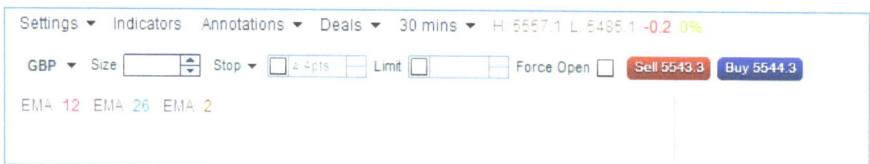

Fig 74, Trading directly from the chart

The procedure is quite easy and self explanatory. First enter the size of trade (the amount you want to bet). Then enter to stop loss you want in the next box but note that you should tick the small box to the left if you want a guaranteed stop. In the next box, enter the limit that you want (the amount of profit) and finally click buy or sell depending on which direction you want to trade.

After having tried it for a short while, I now prefer this new system as you can instantly open a trade whilst still looking at the chart instead of flicking back to the main IG interface. However, if you prefer you can still use the main IG page to place your trades as described earlier.

Another feature I like is that as soon as you open a trade, your stop loss, your opening position and your profit limit position as well as the current position are automatically shown on the chart as shown in Fig 75 as soon as you open a trade. This immediately gives you a visual representation of what is happening which is very useful. However, to close a trade, you still have to do this via the main page as previously described.

In this example, I am selling so the stop loss position is indicated by a red dotted line above the solid red line (opening position) and the profit limit is indicated by the blue dotted line below it. At this instant in time, the bottom of the red candle is just below the solid red line (my opening position) so I am in profit at this stage.

Fig 75 New IG chart (FTSE 100)

Note also, that these charts show the MACD with both lines and the histogram (bars) simultaneously.

RISK MANAGEMENT

How much money do I need to start trading?

Unfortunately, the lower the amount of money you can afford to start out with, the harder it is to manage the risk effectively. It is usually recommended that you do not risk more than 2% on any single trade. So if you started with £1,000, the recommendation is that you do not risk using more than £20 to trade with and at this level it is difficult if not impossible to make a satisfactory profit.

So what should we start with - £1,000, £2,000, £5,000? In the real world, most people would have difficulty in raising £1,000 so should we not bother to consider trading at all?

All I can say is that I have made some substantial profits using much lower trading funds than £1,000 and based on the *Visual Forex Trader* system you could start with £200/200$, providing you are careful and only trade on the signals that have been described. To start at this level, you must use a low stake to start with – 50p in the case of the EUR/USD and don't touch anything else. Of course your risk is higher than using a higher starting fund but it is possible to make decent profits if you are careful.

But don't forget, it is also possible to lose all your trading funds so you must be able to afford to lose this amount in the event of things going wrong. However, if you can afford to risk this sum and are prepared to build up your funds slowly then you stand a very good chance of succeeding.

To stand the best chance of succeeding, **use a trading strategy and stick to it**. Do not make irrational, emotional or wild decisions. Just keep calm and stick to your plan. When they have been stopped out, a lot of traders feel cheated or angry and try to claw back what they have lost by immediately opening new trades with higher stakes and believe me - this is a recipe for disaster so don't try it!

Managing stop losses

Several times in this book, I have mentioned the high danger of losing money if you do not have a satisfactory trading strategy. You **must** have a trading plan before you open any trade and then stick to it after the trade is opened.

If you let emotion rule over your plan, it is all too easy to succumb to the overwhelming urge when you are close to being stopped out, to increase your stop loss and keep on doing this when you should have let the stop loss do its job – close your trade.

You selected your stop loss before you started to trade as part of your strategy knowing it was there to protect you so let it stop you out as intended when things go against you as you planned.

I mentioned previously that slippage is quite likely to occur when you leave your trade going overnight with certain instruments – those that have set opening and closing times – like the FTSE 100. Fig 76 shows what can happen when you trade this instrument outside these times using the spread betting company's simulated trading facility – or as in this case leave your trade active during the time the FTSE was closed.

Fig 76 Slippage of approx 136 pips on FTSE 100

The FTSE closed at 5551.4 on the 30th December 2011 at 9:00 pm and when it re-opened on 3rd Jan 2012, it had slipped to a high of 5687.6 representing 136 pips. which at £2 per pip, amounts to £272. Now let's say you set a non guaranteed stop loss of 60 pips – thinking this would be adequate. The net result would have been that you would have been stopped out as soon as the FTSE re-opened at 5646 meaning that you would lose 5646.1- 5561.4 = 85 pips as opposed to the 60 pips you set. In other words you would have lost £175 instead of the £120 you allowed.

The moral in this tale is that when trading the FTSE 100, you should always try to stop trading at the close of trading at 4:30 pm GMT. Firstly, it avoids the considerably higher spread and secondly, it avoids the situation illustrated in Fig 76.

If you must leave your trade running on the FTSE overnight then use *a guaranteed stop* as discussed earlier as this will stop you out at the stop loss you intended regardless of slippage.

I should remind you here that the EUR/USD is not prone to slippage of this scale as the market remains open continuously from Sunday night to Friday night. However, if you leave a trade open between Friday night and Sunday night, then slippage will still be likely to occur.

Ok. Here's the punch line it's quite simple. Try not to leave open trades running when the spread betting company's trading platform is closed. If you feel you can't avoid leaving a trade open, then use a **guaranteed stop loss.**

The sign of a successful trader is to cut any losses that start getting out of control so that when your losses start mounting, as painful as it seems, close these trades and you will live to fight another day. Bad traders run up high losses in the hope that the market will reverse and also take their profits far too early. However, if you faithfully follow the strategies I have provided you will be far more successful.

Up until recently, with intraday trading you had to stay by your computer to continuously check for the trading signals. However, as all the spread betting companies I have mentioned offer apps for you mobile phone, this means you no longer have to do this and you can now trade direct from your mobile when you are on the move which I find very convenient.

Please note, however, you **must** have access to your trading account at all times to take advantage of the strategy in the *Visual Forex Trader* otherwise you will miss many of the trading signals and hence profit making opportunities.

USING LIMIT ORDERS

I have left this topic until last as *limit orders* are not used with *Visual Forex Trader* strategy. My system is based on reacting to the signals presented by the EMA and MACD indicators. I am mentioning it now for two reasons

1. You may simply be wondering what it is and how it works
2. There may occasionally times when you could use a limit order to your advantage.

IG offers the following explanation of the use of a limit order.

'A Limit order is an instruction to deal (either 'buy' or 'sell') if a price becomes more favourable.

For example, if we were quoting the March FTSE 100 at 6746/6752, you might place a Limit order to 'buy' if the dealing price of our quotation (in this case the 'offer' price) drops to 6730.

A Limit order will be triggered if, at any time inside or outside market hours, the relevant dealing price of our quotation is at, or through, the Limit level.'

Right, let's explain this in plain English and with a practical example. Look at Fig 77. Up until now the EUR/USD has been moving along quite happily within a nice steady predictable cycle. All of a sudden it has leaped upwards after a breakout and if we had have been trading this, our stop loss would have been triggered and closed any open selling trade we had – yes?

Hopefully, you will had had an opposing buying trade open at the same time so that you would have picked up all this nice juicy profit. Hence our trading strategy has worked our well since you have taken the profit while stopping the selling loss from getting any bigger.

However, another look at the chart where the indicators show that the current price level is far too high and **overbought** and using my elastic band analogy, the price will be bound to come back down again before long. In view of this we could take advantage of it by using a **limit order**.

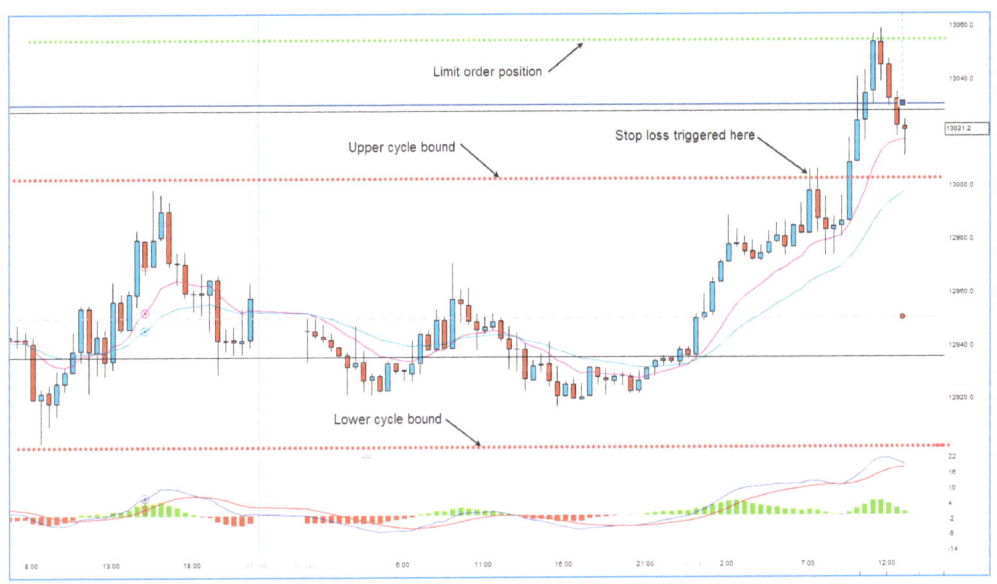

Fig 77 Opening a limit order on the EUR/USD

As usual, the red dotted lines indicate the upper and lower cycle bounds and in accordance with out trading strategy, when the breakout occurred, it triggered our selling stop loss when the price broke through the upper bound. We continue to take the profit from our opposing buying trade but the price still seems to be going up and knowing the price has to drop back again at some point, we open a limit order to try and take advantage of this.

At this point we don't know how much higher the price is going to rise but we could open a limit order that starts a selling trade when the price falls back down to the level indicated by the green dotted line. Nothing will happen until the price hits this level and the selling trade is triggered.

In the meantime we continue to take the profit from our buying trade until it starts to stutter and then we close this trade. But at this instant in time, we still don't know how high the price is going to go. For example, it may carry on upwards after a brief pause but at some point it must change direction and eventually trigger our selling trade as the price falls to the limit order position.

As you can see, in this case, the price did not in fact go up very much higher and started to reverse direction and triggered or selling trade as it passed through the limit order position providing us with another profit as it continued downwards.

The question is: How do we know where to put the limit order position? The answer is not straightforward. It has to be low enough to give a reasonable chance that it will continue downwards once it has been triggered. However, we can see from our indicators that a vertex is about to appear on the EMA's and that the MACD D is about to crossover.

Therefore if we set the limit order to apply just a little bit further down from this position, it looks fairly certain that the price is going to drop further than this for a while.

So why not open a selling trade in the ordinary way if we think this is going to happen? The answer is that we are protected against the price hesitating and rising again. It is only when the limit order is activated that the selling trade is opened.

Another example of the use of a limit order is when we actually want to open a trade after we have switched our computer off. This demonstrated in Fig 78.

Fig 78 FTSE 100

We can see here that there is an upward trend here as indicated by the arrow and it would be reasonable to assume that this trend will continue. We could take a flier and buy at the current price but if the price fell, we could lose heavily and as we are not at our computer we can't do anything to top it, except put on a stop loss.

On the other hand, we could place a limit order to buy at the position of the green dotted line. If the price reached this level, the trend will be continuing and we should make a profit.

These are just two examples of the use of limit orders but I would recommend that you do not use these until you ate thoroughly familiar with trading in the normal way and have gained a lot more experience.

SUMMARY

- Start with a small stake until you get the feel of trading
- Begin with the EUR/USD and avoid trading on volatile markets
- Follow the system I have described, in the order listed in the book
- Don't be impatient when the market slows
- Take things easy at first until you have gained more experience
- Do not spend more than you can afford to lose
- Read the manual through several times before you start and make sure you understand everything in it.
- Start by paper trading without risking real money
- Begin with the advantageous lower stakes offered by IG Index or the simulated trading using fictitious money offered by Capital Spreads.

Finally remember that it is easy to lose money when spread betting and you must approach it carefully as there are risks that are involved. Never spend more than you can afford to lose.

www.ingramcontent.com/pod-product-compliance
Lightning Source LLC
Chambersburg PA
CBHW050812290526
45792CB00001B/81